TOK258

Morgan Winner at Le Mans

50th Anniversary Edition

Ronnie Price

Richard Shepherd-Barron

First published in 2005

© Copyright 2005, 2012
Ronnie Price

Paperback ISBN 978-1-78092-079-5
ePub ISBN 978-1-78092-080-1
PDF ISBN 978-1-78092-081-8

Published in the UK by MX Publishing
335 Princess Park Manor, Royal Drive, London, N11 3GX
www.mxpublishing.co.uk

Cover design by Martin Chiles

Dedicated to the memory of Chris Lawrence who really believed TOK could win

Chris Lawrence at Le Mans in 2002 with TOK 258 and the Morgan Aero 8 GTN which competed in the 24hr race. Chris did a lap of honour in TOK.
(Picture courtesy of Malvern Link)

INTRODUCTION AND CREDITS

When I first conceived the idea of a second edition it was to celebrate the 50th anniversary of the epic Morgan win at Le Mans in 1962 – a golden celebration. But now I should also like to dedicate it to the memory of Chris Lawrence the driving force behind that victory and so many other achievements in and outside motorsport.

This second edition is very different, one of the main reasons being the involvement of Richard Shepherd-Barron as co-author.

As the co-driver at that 1962 race he was literally in the driving seat and brought TOK over the finish line. So it is a great honour to have him so closely involved in the Golden Anniversary edition.

We have split the book into two parts. Part one is virtually the original; and part two based on Richard's own story. An excellent DVD 'BEHIND THE PITS – personal memories' is based on the original cine-camera filming done by his wife Penny, with commentary by Richard, and covers his racing in the period including special focus on the Le Mans race and practice.

There are new photos and material in this celebratory edition from Roger Tatton, The Morgan Sports Car Club archivist, and Machiel Kalf leading collector of TOK 258 history and memorabilia.

Inevitably there is variance between the different accounts: for example who attended the May practice; and did TOK drive to Le Mans or go by trailer. But we decided that rather than trying to 'homogenize' the stories these 'nuggets' add spice and mystery to what is now virtually an historic motorsport legend!

The first credit must go to the Morgan Motor company for continuing to develop and build such splendid cars; and to the ongoing Morgan success in motorsport internationally, classic vintage events and in the heart of motorsport, the hundreds of club events which are regularly held by enthusiasts round the world.

When working on the first edition I was indebted to Christopher Lawrence and his delightful wife Carrie, who made me so welcome at their Hereford home. Much of the detail in the original book and much of the background comes from a few fascinating hours talking with Chris. Sadly Chris died on August 13th 2011. It is nice to recall that Morgan enthusiasts gathered to pay tribute to him at Goodwood in June 2005. On that occasion I had the pleasure of meeting Richard Shepherd-Barron for the first time and he subsequently sent me his reminiscence of the great race adding valuable insight to the story. The Lawrence tribute at Goodwood was orchestrated by Dutch Morgan historian Machiel Kalf who provided invaluable reports and data for the first edition and now additional material for the new edition from his unique collection. Rick Bourne who owned and cared for TOK at the time of the first edition generously gave access to his collection of photographs. Original photographs have been supplied by Ted Walker of Ferret Photographics. The deputy editor of "Motor Sport", Gordon Cruickshank, kindly took time to research their archives and turned up "Jenks" somewhat typically laconic comments.

I also got important background from two very readable histories of the Morgan marque – one by Brian Laban and the other by Gregory Houston Bowden. Skimming various reports in the Morgan Sports Car Club magazine "Miscellany", especially in relation to the 2002 and 2004 Le Mans Classic events, was highly instructive. I'm always impressed by the quality and metronomic reliability of that publication.

The September 2002 edition of "Malven Link" – the Morgan Company newsletter at that time – was also a very good source of information. In fact it was probably the report in that issue on the Le Mans 2002 Classic – and the interview with Chris Lawrence – which first provoked the thought that there should be a specific book dedicated to TOK's 1962 victory.

The Morgan Sports Car Club does such an excellent job in bringing together the many Morgan enthusiasts around the world through "Miscellany" and activities: the backbone of Morgan ownership. Their archives have provided a splendid collection of new photos.

I owe a thank you to Richard and Helen Thorne who introduced me to Morganeering with such positive enthusiasm and support. And it was always interesting talking with John MacDonald about racing Morgans; he had a special success himself at Nurburgring.

As an author I must state that I have tried to reproduce faithfully the information I have assembled: if any of the facts are wrong or misleading, please forgive me. It is almost fifty years since TOK 258 did her stuff at Le Mans and all memory suffers from time. It is certainly not my intention to malign anyone or anything! So sorry if I have done so.

I have also given full credit for photographs whenever details have been available. Apologies for any omissions. I must thank Lucy Cordeiro who has slaved over a hot computer to convert my scribble into text for the first edition; and Martin Chiles for the new cover-design and all his work on the compilation of this anniversary edition.

My publisher Steve Emecz is always most supportive; his company MX Publishing is one of the most advanced publishers in the electronic field. My last book Man Made Magic was on Amazon within three days of publication, and on Kindle not much later.

Ronnie Price

CONTENTS

PART ONE

By Ronnie Price

FOREWORD BY CHARLES MORGAN

As a ten year old I completely idolised Chris Lawrence and Richard Shepherd-Barron. Their Le Mans result was the stuff of schoolboy dreams; drive to the 24 hour race in a semi standard car to battle it out with the wealthy Ferrari and Porsche teams to win their class and drive home. They were my superheroes and gave me all the street cred I needed as a member of the Morgan family battling it out in a competitive playground at school.

Before the race during the Easter holiday I had a personal experience with the spare British Racing Green and Cream car, 170 GWP. My father took me out in it to test the top speed on the Ross Spur motorway. In the days before speed limits at just over 130mph the tread of one of the rear tyres started to peel away from the steel core. The loud detonation and following flapping noise forced us to slow down pretty fast. This experience made my admiration for the bravery of Chris and Richard on the Mulsanne Straight very vivid.

When Chris joined me at the Morgan Motor Company 35 years later to engineer the suspension for a new Morgan the spirit of Le Mans 1962 was still all there. We wanted to prove that a car that was a comfortable high speed long distance tourer could race at Le Mans and cover itself in glory. So far the performance of Chris and Richard in TOK has not been equalled but we are not about to give up and Morgan definitely has unfinished business at Le Mans.

I would recommend this book to anyone. It is the story of how skill and personal determination can beat the most elaborate, expensive and sophisticated machinery, the story of David versus Goliath. I warmly hope that it inspires the reader to try and achieve their own personal dreams.

Charles Morgan
Chairman, Morgan Motor Company

CHAPTER ONE

TOK 258 – Morgan Victory at Le Mans

You might say that this was a very British affair in the best traditions of "Boy's Own Paper" – a ripping yarn. A tiny team with modest support and limited resources coming up against the cream of well funded and experienced international race teams with legendary factory drivers is a very appealing piece of imagery. A small six years old traditional English sports car designed in the 30's competing with the latest technology in suspension systems, slippery body shapes and highly developed racing engines. But dig a bit deeper and you may throw-up a somewhat different slant to the story. The basics of the Morgan sports car with its unique build and suspension created by founder HFS, provided, and still provides, an exceptional platform for a performance car. Marry this with permitted "Lawrencetune" modifications and expert tuning and you have a very good racing machine. Chris Lawrence, the master tuner and driver who took TOK to victory, was confident from the outset that it was the quickest two litre car in the race and could certainly win unless they were unlucky enough to hit trouble. And it would have to be very bad luck because TOK is a strong car. Chris and his co-driver Richard Shepherd-Barron were both experienced and successful sports-car drivers and had both won championships. They had both enjoyed considerable success in big continental races. So surprisingly perhaps to outsiders this was a stronger team than it may have looked to be on the surface. It is thought provoking if a little fanciful to compare it with the Battle of Britain. It is common to see that portrayed as a miracle – the glory of "the few". But again underpinning the miracle there was an array of impressive technology and human skills. Professional pilots of exceptional ability very well trained and led. Radar the ultimate secret weapon, and of course the superb Hurricane and Spitfire with awesome eight-gun firepower. While over home territories RAF pilots who baled out could soon be back with their squadrons, Luftwaffe aircrew would become prisoners of war.

Looked at objectively a win for the TOK at Le Mans in 1962 like the win for the RAF in 1940, was not quite so unlikely and romantic as it may seem at first sight. Still, TOK's win was a splendid achievement and Morgan recognised its importance in re-enforcing the fundamental link between the famous brand and sporting success. Perhaps it also helped to endorse the policy of continuing with the classic body shape and not being drawn into the trend for streamlined enclosures. So let's raise a glass to TOK for helping to keep Morgan cars looking distinctive as they should, and for its help in preserving the future of the Morgan sports car.

Sporting achievement had always been at the heart of the Morgan ethos – providing the enthusiastic driver with a rewarding-to-drive sports car at a competitive price. This tradition goes right back to the three-wheeler win in the French Grand Prix for the cycle-car class in 1913. However Morgan's sporting wins have not just been at big name events. They have in a sense a more valuable history of winning across a wide-range of motor sport activities: trials, rallies, hill-climbs, sprints and club racing at a variety of circuits around the world. The Morgan concept makes it possible for ordinary club owners to take part with modest budgets and in cars which they can run on an everyday basis.

The Aero 8 has already done well in the competition continuing the tradition of beating Porches in GT competition. Nor has it done too badly at Sebring, Silverstone, Le Mans and Bahrain. The modern range of Morgan cars – and the new three-wheeler! – is mouthwatering. And the presence of Morgans at a motoring occasion inevitably brings a touch of class and style to hint at a glorious bygone era in automobile history, which can still be enjoyed today. Now in 2012, the Morgan name is back at Le Mans with two Oak-Pescarolo Judd-engined LMP2 cars. Announcing this earlier in the year, Charles Morgan said: "Whilst Morgan sports cars enjoy a great history we have also gained a reputation for pioneering new technology, and I believe LMP2 represents a superb proving ground in which to develop innovative new methods".

CHAPTER TWO

Getting The Official Entry

When Chris Lawrence went to Le Mans for the '62 practice weekend the car had already been formally accepted for the race. And he was en route to achieving a long time ambition to race at Le Mans. This had been given a real fillip by the performance of TOK in 2 litre international competition, especially in the 60 and 61 TT at Goodwood. He thought originally he was going to start at the 1961 Le Mans race– not in TOK but in XRXI, the pale blue Morgan Plus Four he was hoping to run under a Lawrencetune entry. With the Morgan's excellent success record at Nurburgring, Spa and elsewhere, Chris and Richard felt confident about securing an entry at Le Mans. The car went through all the scrutineering – 2 days and 24 stages – without any problems. As Chris tells it, they were just waiting for the official ACO approval stamp to dry off (it was a painted stencil), when a small deputation arrived and spoke confidentially with the monsieur who had painted on the stamp. After some debate he returned and advised Chris that the car had failed. He then wiped away his stamp. It seems the reason given was that the Morgan was thought to be an old pre-war car that had been re-sprayed, fitted with disc brakes and generally tarted up and was not therefore eligible. However a deep suspicion persists that the rejection was a put-up-job engendered by the political pressure from a rival factory team, Triumph, which feared the embarrassment of being beaten by the little Morgan, using a modified version of their own Triumph engine. The offer which the Le Mans organisers couldn't refuse is reputed to have been along the lines of "you can have three factory cars ... or one elderly Morgan privately entered ... Your choice". Whatever the reason the Morgan wasn't allowed to start.

However, in 1962 after further Morgan international success, the TOK 258 entry was apparently welcomed. Nevertheless Chris Lawrence wasn't overly confident that it might not again be rejected at the last minute on some pretext and although he did all the entry documentation himself he was very relieved to have it entered officially by the Morgan factory. As an official works entry it acquired a different status. Moreover being a Morgan works entry it had the substantial support of Jacques Savoye, the French Morgan agent who had a lot of influence at Le Mans.

The factory support included a colour change and there is an interesting story behind that. TOK had always been red and Chris Lawrence had it repainted in burgundy red, including the hard top. He explains that it was an expensive high quality job and the car looked really smart. It appeared in this livery at the Le Mans test weekend. Subsequently one of the French race officials, M. Accat of the ACO, wrote to the Morgan company as the official entrant congratulating them on the car's appearance and its performance, but asking them to re-finish it in British Racing Green for the race. Chris Lawrence had spent a lot on the burgundy repaint and refused to paint TOK again. He said he couldn't afford it. So Peter Morgan agreed to do so. However this created a petit problem...

Morgan had a company policy of keeping model types well defined. But to improve the aerodynamics and reduce weight Chris wanted to fit a low-line 4/4 body on TOK's Plus Four chassis. The story told by Chris is that Morgan wouldn't sell him a 4/4 body, so he did it surreptitiously by buying parts piece by piece from the stores. Obviously the body change would be picked up when TOK went to be painted green. In the end TOK was taken to the Pickersleigh Road works, early in the morning and left outside the paint shop in the forlorn hope that no one would notice the change in body type! Chris told his foreman to leave it there and "then run like hell to get the train back". However, in the end all was resolved amicably and satisfactorily with the ingenious solution of the "Hybrid" being associated with a limited edition range, the "plus Four Super Sport" of which ultimately 101 were sold. There may be other versions of this story...

Christopher Lawrence recalls that Morgan had done a magnificent job in re-finishing TOK, which did the Morgan marque proud with its handsome elegant stance when lining up the start of the race. For the race the Morgan factory provided two experienced mechanics; and loaned a back-up car – a British Racing Green Plus Four – reg. 170 GWP – to be used for spare parts. This was in fact the factory prototype and demonstrator for what become the Plus 4 Super Sports. Both cars were driven to Le Mans for the race, or did TOK go in the specially converted caravan-trailer? It was a small team – six including the drivers – but smart looking and well prepared. The Lawrencetune Morgan team had special racing overalls from Dunlop. "I just tucked my trousers into my socks in the good old days" quipped Christopher Lawrence.

There are various stories about getting TOK and the support car 170 GWP to Le Mans. Did the drivers, travelling from different starting points, fail to meet up at Dover? Was either TOK 258 or 170 GWP left in a lay-by with a note in the window "small problem, please bring on to Le Mans"? It doesn't really matter, but it does add to an already colourful story, although Richard covers this later.

After the vicissitudes of '61, at last the game was now on and the drivers were quietly confident about having a good race. Morgan were also hoping for a good outcome and the workforce was rooting for TOK. Managing Director, Peter Morgan, was there himself to provide top level support yet probably none of them could have been hoping for a class win – except perhaps Chris Lawrence.

CHAPTER THREE

The Drivers

Chris Lawrence has said that as a racing driver he had three main ambitions: to be invited to become a member of the British Racing Drivers' Club; to race at Indianapolis – the 500 'brickyard'; and to drive at Le Mans. He never made Indianapolis but no doubts about achieving the other goals.

He started his engineering career as a professional Naval Officer training at Dartmouth, later becoming a Royal Navy Engineer officer qualified as a mechanical engineer. By 1952 he had been badly bitten by the motor racing bug and eventually brought himself out of his naval commission and began working at ROTAX, part of the Lucas Group with strong connections to the automotive sector.

He had a few seasons with a mix of cars, Bugatti, MG, AFN, but eventually he decided that he had to get serious. He had recently become engaged to be married and things were pretty tight. As he puts it himself, "No car and no money". He focused on marque racing and after considering Austin Healey and Triumph, picked Morgan as the car for the job. In 1958 he bought TOK 258, a two year old Morgan Plus Four from Performance Cars in London for £650. After some preparation he entered his first race in TOK at Aintree which was then a premier British Circuit. Historically speaking, this wasn't his very first Morgan race – he had raced a JAP three wheeler Morgan in the early 50's. He did not enjoy success at the Aintree race but it wasn't long before he did. He took the lap record at Goodwood and 2nd place. The results in the first season were positive enough for him to feel encouraged about the next season's prospects. He had formed a specialist tuning company: "Lawrencetune Engines Ltd", in November 1959 with ex ROTAX colleagues who had been helping part-time with TOK thorough 1958/9. They were Leslie Fagg, John Harvey and Len Bridge.

In 1959 he put a new camshaft in TOK and modified the cylinder head. That year he won the Freddie Dixon marque championship with TOK a remarkable feat in their second season together.

TOK 258 at Aintree 1961 – Driven by Chris Lawrence
(Picture courtesy of Ferret Fotographics www.ferret1.co.uk)

Initially in the marque series he claims he was helped by an ingenious starting technique for the Le Mans style starts, developed with colleagues for ROTAX. He was able to leave the car with the hand brake on, with a special solenoid switched on. He sprinted over to car, jumped in, depressed the clutch and selected first, causing the engine to fire; and he was smartly away ahead of the field. This saved seconds and helped him to a first place. A special race committee set up by B.A.R.C., the marque series organisers considered this. They allowed the wins up until that time to stand but developed new regulations to prohibit the system in future. Still ... it was a good run! Of the 22 races he entered in 1959 he won 19 – an astonishing statistic even by Schumacher standards. In 1960 he almost won the 2litre class in TT (at Goodwood). He was running in a good 3rd position and then passed, first Jo Bonnier, then Graham Hill, both in Porsche Carrera-Abarth cars. However, during a pit stop to change the "Seagrave" premier tread tyres, cheap and sticky, the starter motor jammed. He replaced it himself because he had only one mechanic who was re-fuelling the car. While he was busily engaged in this tricky task and under pressure, he became somewhat irritated. Radio commentator John Bolster in his deer-stalker hat was interrogating him, vigorously waving a microphone in his face while he worked against time. When he eventually made a rapid exit from the pits he, erm ... unfortunately ran over Bolster's toe. Apparently this didn't endear him to the intrepid reporter. On the other hand "Jenks" the famous "Motor Sport' magazine correspondent picked Chris out in 1955 as having potential; and motor journalist, Dennis Jenkins, was not given to facile praise. The occasion was the 1955 Bank Holiday meeting – the "Annerley Trophy Event", a race for 1100cc sports racing cars. The field included 3 works

Lotuses and two works Coopers. There were two heats and a final; Chris came third in the final driving a 1933 vintage N/K MG Magnette against very competitive contemporary machinery.

Chris Lawrence says that it was TOK's competitiveness with the Porsches in the 1960 TT at Goodwood which made him realise the potential of the Morgan for a really big win in its class. Apparently it also gave Porsche pause for thought although the real reaction came later in 1962 after the Le Mans win and losing the Nurburgring lap record to Morgan. The story is that they brought out the 904 ahead of plan and to do so may allegedly have played games with mock-ups for homologation. Surely not.

This was the period in which Chris Lawrence really became a professional – when he moved on from being an amateur driver and an amateur tuner. Another impressive run came in 1961. The Italian Grand Prix had a warm up prior to the main event called "The Coppa InterEuropa". This was a three hour sports car race which was reckoned to be a Porsche benefit. Chris drove XRXI but to give his colleagues Les Fagg and Len Bridge a "fun" drive, they also took TOK with a 2.2 engine. They were doing very well in TOK, not far behind Chris in XRXI, until a niggling but persistent oil leak forced them to be disqualified.

XRXI had been purchased from Morgan as an untrimmed basic car, "at a very good price". It had a secret weapon in the form of a 22 gallon fuel tank. The pale blue car was acquired for a special reason. Chris Lawrence's family, especially his mother, wanted him to stop racing and were putting a lot of pressure on him. Using the fact that a debenture had been set up to secure a bank loan to help expand his company Lawrencetune, the family got an injunction restraining him from racing TOK 258. To get around this, Chris arranged for another driver with whom he had teamed up for 61/62, to enter a different Morgan – XRXI under the co-driver's name. This was Richard Shepherd-Barron, who in due course shared the 62 Le Mans drive. Richard was also another sports car driver and took part in the "Autosport" Championship in 59/60 with an Alfa Romeo Giulietta "Sprint Veloce". Richard retired from racing after the 62 Le Mans win, and now writes for farming, business and motoring magazines.

Back to 1961 and the Coppa InterEuropa at Monza. The capacious 22 gallon tank of XRXI played an important tactical role. The Lawrencetune team made a big show of practising re-fuelling from the then standard "milk churns". They did this hour after hour under the scrutiny of Porsche who studying it all carefully concluded that the Lawrencetune Morgan would probably twice stop for fuel. Come the race and Chris in the Morgan was running third in the two litre class, nine seconds behind Edgar Barth who was first in a Porsche Carrera-Abarth and Von Hanstein who was second. With 45 minutes to go, the Porches hadn't stopped and at the same time, Chris heard a change in his engine note and had to reduce power. Eventually the Porsches came in to re-fuel and he took the lead. The Porsche team wasn't bothered – they were waiting for him to stop to refuel... but with the 22 gallon tank he didn't need to. Finally with not much time left the pfennig dropped and Porsche in panic had to put on the pace. Chris took a chance on his engine-noise and also pulled out the stops speeding up again. Edgar Barth just managed to get by before the end of race but Chris hung on for third place behind Von Hanstein. Thereafter Porsche treated Morgan with more than a little respect.

Chris reminisces that the Morgan was very good at Monza's 'Lesmo' which was a combination of two corners. He could take it in one, long classic four-wheel drift using the car's excellent balance and neutral steering. Apparently this driving style was much appreciated by the knowledgeable Italian "Tifosi", who enthusiastically waved their programmes when Chris drifted past.

Chris Lawrence had the very special experience of racing at the original awe inspiring "Nurburgring" and recalls getting a valuable tip from Richard's friend, Jim Clark whom he had got to know at various meetings. He was trying to get in a good time but found a particular stretch of the long and difficult circuit very problematical. Jim took him round in a road-car and gave him advice on the difficult uphill stretch. The result was a dramatic drop in Chris's lap time, a 10 seconds' saving. When measured against current F1 margins counted in milli-seconds that sounds a huge gain, but although it was very respectable, it has to be reckoned against the average times recorded for the extremely long "Nurburgring" laps. Nevertheless, this sudden significant improvement in lap times, surprised the co-driver: he couldn't work out what he was doing wrong and what Chris was doing right. After letting him stew a while, Chris explained his secret and team amity was restored.

Despite opposition from his mother – it seems clear that Chris Lawrence has racing in his blood. In fact, His father raced motorcycles at Brooklands in the 20s and founded the Vintage Motorcycle Club. Later he rode AJS racing bikes and Chris did some motorcycle grass track racing; he claims to be the only sports car driver who has been round Brands Hatch in the wrong direction – anti clockwise – and on the grass, albeit on two wheels.

Although there were of course two drivers at the 62 Le Mans race, and Richard Shepherd-Barron fully played his part doing 12 hours out of 24 hours, indeed finally taking TOK over the line for the finish at 4pm, it is Chris Lawrence who is so closely linked to TOK and identified with the win. It was his belief, his dream, his technical skills and commitment which drove forward the initial project and justified the crucial support of the Morgan factory in securing the entry and providing back-up for the race. The Le Mans '62 win was not, of course, the end of the TOK story: by the end of that year the combination of TOK and Chris had taken the lap records for the "up to 2 litre" class for every major UK Racing Circuit. These records stood for several years. The details of the Chris Lawrence career in automotive design, race car engineering and as a racing driver are summarised in the appendix to this book.

CHAPTER FOUR

The Car

When TOK won its class at Le Mans in 1962 its fundamental design characteristics actually went back to 1934. Girder chassis, ash wooden body frame, aluminium paneling, sliding pillar suspension – still classic Morgan characteristics today. TOK's success at Le Mans and other famous circuits and road races seems to be based on two major factors; the quality and effectiveness of the original Morgan design and the development and tuning by the highly talented Chris Lawrence who had the benefit of driving TOK as well as engineering her!

Chris Lawrence bought TOK 258 in 1958, already two years old. Trying to break into serious racing after six years in club racing, Chris had decided that the route to go was British marque racing – (Austin Healeys, Triumphs, MGs) The National Marque Championship. Significantly he had also decided that the Morgan Plus Four was the best car for the job.

It was a good choice and over the next few years the partnership enjoyed considerable success. It began with taking the Marque Series lap record at Goodwood shortly after he acquired TOK. They didn't win that race but it augured well and next year, and as already recorded, in 1959 they won 19 out of 22 races in the Marque Championship to win the Freddie Dixon (of Riley Fame) Championship. TOK has the distinction of never failing to finish a Freddie Dixon marque race. In 1960 there was a lap record in the two-litre GT class at Silverstone and class win in the Goodwood TT. The success in the Coppa Inter

Europa 2-litre class at Monza confirmed Chris Lawrence's view that a good result at Le Mans would be possible and that became the target.

TOK being driven by Chris Lawrence at Brands Hatch – August 1963
(Picture courtesy Ferret fotographics www.ferret1.co.uk)

Le Mans 62 was not the end of the successful partnership because in 1963 they had wins at Spa, Nurburgring, Dijon and Clermont-Ferrand. TOK also won the Freddie Dixon trophy in 1965. Although for the 1962 Le Mans race, the basics were unchanged, a considerable amount of work was done by Lawrencetune to prepare for a demanding twenty-four hour high speed endurance event. A 4/4 body replaced the Plus 4 body. The 4/4 was lower – creating less drag – and lighter. A further aid to drag reduction was the complete enclosure underneath the car with all apertures being covered up. The finishing touch on the streamline front was to fit specially made aluminium one piece top. Chris Lawrence explains that this also aided stability at speed because it moved the centre of pressure to the rear of the car, a form of down force. The Morgan has good inherent chassis characteristics being well-balanced and with neutral steering – no oversteer or understeer. It has a neat turn-in ability and good traction out of corners; it performs well in a controlled four-wheel drift. The 45% angle at which the Koni shock absorbers were set at the rear, helped to minimize wheel tramp. Stronger stub axles were used to combat the stress of higher cornering speeds.

The engine was the Triumph TR3 used at that time in Morgan Plus 4 cars. In its standard form it produced 92 BHP. It was originally derived from the engine used by Standard Triumph in the Ferguson tractor engine and later for the Standard Vanguard saloon car. The engine used at Le Mans was based on the Super Sports engines which were being prepared for Morgan by Lawrencetune for the new Plus Four Super Sports based on the TOK body specification. Lawrencetune eventually delivered more than 100 of these Super Sports engines to the factory. The conversion from the standard TR3 unit entailed a complete strip down; the crank rods, pistons, flywheel, crank pulley were all balanced by Jack Brabham's outfit at Surbiton. There was a 22 hour re-work of the head, and a Lawrence cam profile was done by Reece in Carshalton. The sump was modified to combat oil surge. A cast alloy Weber cooler connection block was deployed between block and oil filter head. A Lawrencetune exhaust system was used. For the Le Mans engine there was a lot more work on the cylinder head including the location of valve centres. The standard TR3 produced 92 BHP, the Super Sports 120 BHP and TOK's Le Mans engine 134 BHP.

In 1962 the engine would have cost £900 – a considerable sum at that time. The installation of Weber carburation was undertaken with the help of Keith Duckworth of Cosworth fame. In 1960 he had originally helped Lawrencetune with the use of Weber carburettors when they were preparing cars for Formula Junior. Chris Lawrence recalls that it was the result of this work on the engine which took the power output to 134 BHP at 5750 RPM. For a car weighing some 800 kilos and with a low drag body this was a very positive power-weight ratio. However, perhaps more significantly the torque was an excellent 140 lbs/ft at 3800 RPM. This meant that the car was very driveable at low engine revolutions and thus less strain was imposed on the engine. In fact a 2.9 final drive ratio was used to make it virtually impossible to over-rev, and in top gear (4th) 5,500 RPM was not exceeded during the Le Mans race. First gear was never used apart from starting and the maximum engine revolutions in the intermediate gears, second and third, did not go above 5200. Another aid to the care of the engine over twenty four hours high speed running, was the installation of an oil cooler adapted from a Supermarine Walrus float-plane. Presumably Chris Lawrence's early career as a naval engineering officer may have played some part in this choice. All the modifications were homologated by the Morgan company and subsequently a number were incorporated in the limited edition Morgan Plus Four Super Sports.

TOK appears regularly at the Le Mans historic revival event which take place at Sarthe every alternate year and always receives a hero's welcome from Le Mans crowd, especially the many Morgan enthusiasts who attend and stay in their own special encampment.

TOK 258 Today – Running in the Le Mans Classic
(Picture Courtesy Rick Bourne, Brands Hatch Morgan)

It's great that an historic car like this should be so well cared for in retirement but can still from time to time strut her stuff and charm her many fans.

TOK Today - Leading an interesting gaggle of cars

CHAPTER FIVE

The Test Weekend

One version is that although TOK was driven to the Sarthe Circuit for the race, she hitched a ride for the May practise in the Lawrencetune motor-home. Another version is that it was the other way round! Either way the motor-home was another vehicle with some history. It was designed by Chris Lawrence's stepfather and built by "Two-Town" caravans in Torquay. It was 20' x 6' but had only one pair of wheels. This enabled it be rocked one way to get the car in; and then levelled up when the car was in place and secured. It also featured six bunks which folded down from the sides. There was a specially reinforced platform at the front to accommodate engines. Not quite current F1 practise but you can see where today's top teams may have got their ideas from. The Lawrencetune mobile-home went to several racing circuits in the late 50s and 60s and apparently became the home from home for many home-sick drivers – names like Jim Clark – and "Lucky" Casner (who was later killed at Le Mans in a Maserati), looking to escape from the pressures of fame.

Le Mans 1962. TOK 258 and the "Travelling Spares" back-up car. Note the specially built team home.
(Picture courtesy of Ferret Fotographics – www.ferret1.co.uk)

Also Aussie Frank Gardner who rudely dropped his shorts – in front of ladies! – on one occasion when getting into racing kit.

The co-driver for the race, Richard Shepherd-Barron went to the practice and see Richard's own story in part Two!

The weather on Saturday was fine but Sunday was atrocious and TOK was very steady in the wet because of her first-class balance and driveability. Greenspot Dunlop tyres had been fitted. Moreover the driver felt confident in wet conditions and was able to get the best out of the car. So much so that spectators were astonished to see the small Morgan keeping close company with a Cunningham E type Jaguar.

Chris was tempted once or twice to overtake the Jaguar but the spray was dense and prudence prevailed. But this close running with a quick E type certainly confirmed that the Morgan was one of the fastest cars on the Le Mans circuit that weekend in those conditions.

The race in June was dry but we can speculate about whether TOK in wet conditions might have achieved even greater things than a class win... after all only 13 cars finished. Perhaps with just a little bit of luck and a shower or two of rain?

Eventually, during the practice on a streaming wet track, Chris – who was testing the limits of the adhesion – lost it in the very slippery conditions, coming out of Arnage. He did a couple of 360 degree pirouettes and thought he'd kept it on the black stuff but TOK trickled off into a small ditch. The good news was that there was no significant damage apart from the oil cooler, which was set low down at the front, getting a bit of a wallop.

No times were required in 1962 for qualification but they were recorded and the tests were really an opportunity for the drivers to try out the cars on the circuit as part of preparation for race day. The car had had performed very well, Lawrencetune and Morgan could be well pleased with the results. However, as ever, practice was a different game from the race. That would be the next, the ultimate test.

CHAPTER SIX

Le Mans

Le Mans is a modern city but with a defined history stretching over almost two thousand years. It certainly pre-dates Roman occupation, although as in many other parts of Europe, the Romans left significant marks of their presence especially in still existing fortifications. It acquired its name in the 1100's having survived onslaught by the Vikings and other marauders. Christianity came early and the great Cathedral is testimony to that. It took 100 years to build. Le Mans has a right royal history too. William the Conqueror was born in the area before later becoming the Duke of Normandy and later of course, King of England.

Le Mans was the actual birthplace of Henry II of England who was the first of the Plantagenets on the English throne. Two of his sons became English Kings – Richard the Lion Heart and John of Magna Carta notoriety. The city experienced a turbulent period in the middle ages but also became a prosperous centre for trade.

The connection with the motor industry began at the end of the 19th century and later, developed substantially when Renault opened a car manufacturing factory in the thirties. The circuit – all thirteen and a half kilometres of it – has also seen a lot of changes and has been the subject of political battles, some of them being head-on conflict between the race organisers, ACO, and FISA in the 90's. The Le Mans race had become famous world-wide and well established long before FISA (now FIA) had begun to take over control of major motor sport activity; and the

ACO was already a powerful force with strong lobby contacts at governmental level. Things came to a head when, the ebullient and colourful Monsieur Balestre, the then president of FISA, was determined to bring the ACO into line and to make the Le Mans 24 hours race conform to international sports car racing rules and requirements. Moreover, FISA was not disinterested in the commercial benefits which were engendered by this world famous motor-race and they really wanted to take it over.

However, the ACO had always adopted a very individualist approach and they were well aware that their twenty-four hours sports car race was a much more valuable asset than any other. The Le Mans 24 hours was unique, probably in fact, with more prestige than any other motor race, and could stand alone. It was on a par with other "French" icons like the Monte Carlo Rally and Monaco Grand Prix. There is something of a parallel with the Isle of Man TT motor-cycle race. It is considered to be too dangerous to be included in an International World Championship series, yet it still remains the premier motor-cycle race in the eyes of enthusiasts. We have to wonder how long Monaco will survive in the Formula One world.

The Balestre – ACO face-out became a national dilemma – with both of the combatants French! Politicians joined in, including the French Minister for Sport. Eventually there was compromise. FISA invoked a new regulation decree that no straight could exceed two kilometres, thus outlawing the famous Le Mans Mulsanne straight which was three times that length. The answer was to install two chicanes which many drivers regard as a hazard rather than a safety device. Drivers used to say that the old straight, without chicanes, was the only place on the circuit where you could relax and 'have a bit of a nap'. However, honour was satisfied – more or less.

Happily all this happened after 1962 so TOK didn't have any chicanery. The map in the appendix at the end of the book is extracted from the original race program, showing the configuration of the circuit at that time.

CHAPTER SEVEN

The Race

The strategy for the race was based on finishing. Chris Lawrence believed that if they could finish they stood a very good chance of securing the two-litre class win; and doing pretty well in the overall ranking. His father had taught him "You can't win unless you finish". Underlying the "must finish" philosophy were some practical disciplines. Test runs had shown that they could do a lap in around 5 minutes, but for the race they set an average lap of 5 mins 7 seconds with the fastest laps during the race at 4 minutes 54.0 seconds for Richard and 4 minutes 54.8 seconds for Chris. Intriguingly "Autosport" in its preview of the race reported that in the atrocious weather at the May trials Michael Parkes (Ferrari 12 cylinder, 4 litre) did the best lap in 4 minutes 12 seconds. The Morgan drivers kept to a maximum of 5000rpm in the intermediate gears.

The regulations for 1962 permitted entry of so called "experimental sports car" up to 4 litres capacity. This drew in contenders from Ferrari, Maserati, Jaguar lightweight, E-types and Aston-Martin battling for overall honours; but the entry list included Porsche Carrera-Abarth GTS, Lancia, Simca-Abarth, Alfa Romeo, Sunbeam Alpine, AC Bristol, Austin-Healey, TVR, Marcos and Lotus Elite. There were some big name drivers involved with Barth/Hermann in one Porsche. Sir John Whitmore was in the Healey and Phil Hill/Olivier Gendebien in a Ferrari 330 LM the eventual winner. The hot competition between the bigger, fast, 'experimental sports cars' played well to the Morgan strategy and most of them didn't finish – in fact only 19 cars managed to finish from 55 starters, the Morgan occupying that "lucky" 13th place.

The small Morgan entourage consisted of the two drivers, the Morgan factory mechanics and four Lawrencetune mechanics, also the 'boss' Peter Morgan himself.

Morgan seems to specialise in small efficient teams. At the 2004 Le Mans race they received a special award for their pit-work – to the plaudits of the crowd. In 1962 they used the Lawrencetune motor home but the backup car provided by the factory was actually driven to Le Mans. Chris Lawrence also maintained that TOK itself was driven to Le Mans because they needed to run in the new engine and Moss gearbox which had been fitted to TOK for the race. The team set up in the paddock area "as close to the loo block as possible.

TOK displaying "Its all" at the scene of its 1962 victory – the team site at Le Mans
(Picture courtesy of Ferret Fotographics www.ferret1.co.uk)

Chris Lawrence recalls that he went to have a nice supper in Rennes on the Friday night before the race. He was the guest of Peter Wilson, then chief experimental engineer at Rootes Group who was there in charge of the Sunbeam Alpine entry. Rootes paid for dinner! It was a fairly early night – no wild partying. The driving schedule for the race had been worked out and the drivers split the twenty four hours into three-hour shifts each. They were shared accordingly to the following programme:

Saturday June 3	From	To
Lawrence	4pm	7pm
Shepherd-Barron	7pm	10pm
Saturday (into Sunday)		
Lawrence	10pm	1am
Sunday June 4		
Shepherd-Barron	1am	4am
Lawrence	4am	7am
Shepherd-Barron	7am	10am
Lawrence	10am	1pm
Shepherd-Barron	1pm	4pm

The Morgan had a high capacity tank with a good margin for each 3 hour stint so there was never any need for anxiety about running out of fuel. TOK got a good start: Chris Lawrence had got into training for the traditional sprint across the track and although he couldn't use his special technique developed for marque racing some years earlier, he was one of the first cars away – in fact ninth into the straight "which pissed off a few of the big boys". Chris had talked to one or two people about driving at Le Mans. One name he recalls is Pat Driscoll whom he went to see at his Hayling Island home. Driscoll drove Aston Martins in the thirties; he also raced the "works" baby Austin 750cc overhead camshaft single seater.

Chris Lawrence claims that the race was completely uneventful. The car never missed a beat, the weather was good, and there were no unscheduled stops. Amazingly in twenty four hours flat-out driving, only 28 minutes were spent standing in the pits. Although TOK's engine produced relatively modest brake-horse power its excellent torque was a valuable driver aid. On the 4.5 mile straight, at that time without the modern chicanes, TOK could do about 130mph. This could be pulled up to 135-140mph with the benefit of a good "tow" by slip-streaming one of the really quick cars which was handy, but tricky to handle.

It is interesting to recall that Aston Martin, Ferrari and Maserati with around 350BHP could exceed 170mph on the Mulsanne Straight.

Chris Lawrence doesn't recall any "big moments" or incidents. He did "go like hell in the night". He was quite happy with fast night-driving. He explains that he didn't use marker points at corners or for braking points. He could sustain a level of concentration and react to situations fairly comfortably and so he wasn't too much affected by the limited distance vision at night. "Anyway" he says "if you don't know your way round the track at night after driving around it for several hours in daylight, you shouldn't be racing there." As an example of driver concentration, Christopher Lawrence refers to Charles Morgan driving in a street-race in Helsinki. His co-driver wasn't comfortable with the temporary concrete panel walls which had been erected for the race. He mentioned this to Charles Morgan who said, "what walls?" He'd been concentrating too hard to notice!

The trickiest time at Le Mans was dawn and early morning, with strong sunlight at eye level and patchy fog. The blobs of thick impenetrable mist cropped up at various points around the circuit but didn't stay in one place and so it was virtually impossible to anticipate them. They floated randomly. The driver simply had to drive into the gloom and pray hard that someone wasn't spinning in front of him. Fortunately TOK didn't encounter any errant Ferraris!

There was a moment or two of panic a few hours before the end of the race when one exhaust down-pipe cracked close to the manifold. The pit crew had a look at it during next routine pit stop but decided that it wasn't really serious and not worth spending time trying to repair it. They pressed on without any serious affect being felt: "a couple of hundred revs down and a helluva rattling noise". Still the car was still going well and they could live with that. This blip was immortalised by a typical Dennis Jenkins' cryptic comment in the "Motor Sport 1962" Le Mans report: "minor problems such as broken exhaust manifold; otherwise ran steadily".

So at 4pm on Saturday June 4th 1962 history was made and Richard Shepherd-Barron drove TOK 258 to what was Morgan's finest victory. Two thousand, two hundred and fifty six miles in 24 hours at an average speed – including the scheduled stops – of ninety four miles per hour and at an average fuel consumption of only 29 miles per gallon.

The most famous picture of TOK 258 taking the chequered flag at Le Mans

The Mintex disc brake pads were not changed and only one set of tyres was used. Chris and Richard had a strong memory that they didn't change any tyres at all but others seemed to think that one set was used – in any event testimony to the racing Dunlops of that era and the fine balance of the Morgan chassis.

A very happy pair sat on the Morgan pit counter watching TOK come over the line – Peter Morgan and Chris

Lawrence. For both men it was a significant and far reaching achievement and a major team success. It regenerated the Morgan image and undoubtedly helped them through a tough period of trading. The victory put the seal on Chris Lawrence's career as a driver. It gave him a strong platform for his subsequent international racing success, and a career as a designer and preparer of racing cars.

CHAPTER EIGHT

Celebrating

Forty years on and memories fade. One would like to be able to report on the pomp and ceremony of a glittering prize – giving, with champagne and tuxedos, the flash of diamonds and all those beautiful people. However Chris in his laid-back way played it down. Very nice occasion. He and Richard were feeling really chuffed. Had a few drinks. Collected the cheque – rather important – and the Le Mans finishers' medals. In fact they didn't get the cheque; they got a document which enable them to collect the cheque next day from the ACO offices.

Contrary to other reports Chris Lawrence was clear about what then happened to the money, a not inconsiderable 5500 francs. His co-driver Richard Shepherd-Barron left almost immediately taking the cheque with him and depositing it two days later in the Lawrencetune account at their local National Provincial bank in South Kensington branch in London. It must be recorded that Richard's or Penny's recollection is somewhat different. They don't remember a cheque or any part in depositing it!

Very reasonably at that stage Chris Lawrence felt like a break. It had been a long-term project involving a lot of effort in various ways and then culminating in driving for twelve hours ...so he went to stay with his uncle in what sounds like an idyllic spot: the Villa Poralto on a hill above Cannes. He had the use of his uncle's thirty five foot ketch and for five or six days they sailed around the Med, going over to Corsica at one stage. He remembers in particular that they saw whales during their cruising. (We tend to think of Christopher Lawrence only in terms of his motor racing but he did take part in the 50th anniversary Fastnet race in his 1927 Schooner "La Goleta", winner of Honours back in '27). Cruising the Med was a very enjoyable period of relaxation after the race, but he was soon back at Lawrencetune, where the injection of the winning cheque had been pretty much crucial to the business. As the resumé of his career at the end of this book shows. Christopher Lawrence did not by any means rest on his laurels. Rather than being the pinnacle of his career in motor racing the 1962 Le Mans win with TOK was not only a trigger to long lasting success in racing – in the UK, Europe and he US – but also a career in racing car design and engineering. The latest phase being his key role in the initial development of the Aero 8, in particular the suspension.

But back in 1962 he could be very satisfied with the result of that epic race – a combined operation with TOK, with his co-driver, and with the Morgan factory. Peter Morgan knew that it had been a good decision to back the Lawrencetune project to run TOK at Le Mans. Morgan had always been good at using motor racing to promote its cars and the class win created strong reaction during a time of difficult trading. The quick introduction of the Plus Four "Super Sport" model demonstrates the good commercial and technical acumen which has been a feature of Morgan history and which kept Morgan going when many competitors have faded out.

TOK's victory at the Sarthe Circuit was a big day for Christopher Lawrence and his Lawrencetune company; and a big day for Morgan.

PART TWO

By Richard Shepherd-Barron

FOREWORD BY CHARLES MORGAN

It is almost six years ago since I wrote the introduction to Ronnie Price's little book about the epic win at Le Mans by TOK 258. Since then the legend has continued to grow with TOK appearing at major motor-sport events, now in the capable hands of Keith Ahlers.

Almost unbelievably we are now approaching the 50th anniversary of TOK's triumph and I am delighted to write this introduction to a special celebratory edition.

Le Mans is the oldest sports car race in endurance racing, also the most demanding motor race in the World. It compresses months of action and emotions into a gruelling twenty-four hour period.

Much of the first edition was based on the recollections of Chris Lawrence, the driving force behind the concept, but in this anniversary edition Richard Shepherd-Barron will join Ronnie as co-author to provide an invaluable perspective from the seat of the co-driver who actually brought TOK over the finishing line after twenty-four hours of demanding racing. The teams have to balance economy and performance and conservation of consumable components like tyres, with speed around the track. Today three drivers have to take part, but when TOK competed it was only two. The drama of the race was wonderfully portrayed in the 1964 film, "Un Homme et une Femme" which won an Academy Award, and in the film "Le Mans" starring Steve McQueen.

I am so proud Morgan has been associated with this brilliant event and I hope the relationship between the two famous brands will continue for many years to come.

Charles Morgan
Chairman, Morgan Motor Company

VIEW FROM THE DRIVER'S SEAT

by Richard Shepherd-Barron

I had been racing for a few years in sports and GT races with a Fiat-Abarth and an Alfa Romeo Giulietta Sprint Veloce (also competing in the 1960 1000kms at the Nurburgring in an Ace Ace-Bristol with Bob Staples) I got to know Chris Lawrence here as he was driving an 1100 Lola-Climax with Bill de Selincourt. We all moved on together to Spa for the next weekend and then I did some Formula Junior racing in Italy plus what were really test drives in some FJ races in the UK with Christopher Lawrence's Deep-Sanderson cars. I was actually employed in 1961 by Chris' company – Westerham Motors Ltd in Acton, West London – as a racing and test driver (what excitement – an actual paid driver!). Naturally I was involved also in administration and other work in this small, very busy tuning "shop" which had originally been an upholsterer's premises – old loose tacks were a perpetual problem. Chris bought a new Plus Four Morgan early in 1961 to run as the second car alongside the famous 1956 Plus Four TOK 258. I registered the new car in the Reading licensing office, simply asking if we could have a nice neat number, as one could do in those days for no extra charge The very helpful girl there sorted out XRX 1 which seemed to be just right. We decided to have the car in light blue as we thought it might make the continentals more friendly towards it. Michael Billingham was instrumental in the purchase of an old Marsh and Baxter Austin Loadstar meat pie delivery vehicle which we converted into a transporter and painted it a similar light blue. This was added to the existing transporter operation using a Mk VII Jaguar with a very large caravan which when the car was unloaded doubled up as accommodation with six berths.

Having been to Oulton Park for the Gold Cup meeting where TOK went very well, the first outing on the Continent was in May at Spa-Francorchamps in Belgium for the annual Grand Prix de Spa sports, GT and touring car races. We were delighted to finish a good second in amongst the Porsche Carrera-Abarth cars. Although not as fast in a straight line, the Morgan was more than a match for them on Spa's sweeping fast corners. XRX 1 was fitted with a 2.9 ratio back axle (with Le Mans in our plans) instead of the standard 3.7 and could do over 90mph in second gear! In fact it was rather over-geared but this helped with reliability as we could drive using the strong torque from the 2 litre Triumph TR engine which most certainly helped on the climb back towards the pits. Chris didn't finish with TOK but Peter Marten was 6th with his venerable Plus Four known as "Choc Ices" after a really rather rude joke.

Next stop was the Nurburgring for the 1000kms endurance race. The two cars were very fast although spending a considerable amount of time on each lap off the ground on the very bumpy circuit. Penny came for a lap with me in TOK and said "never again!", although I swear I was only going at about 7/10ths! There were problems with front suspensions stub axles and the factory managed to rush some new ones to us via Michael Billingham and John Jackson who drove out to help in the pits. The two cars at this meeting being driven by Chris, myself, Bob Staples and Peter Marten. As we were at the meeting on the Monday evening (Spa is not far from the Nurburgring), during the week we got to know "Lucky"

Casner and his Camoradi team who were running a Maserati "Birdcage" car for him and Masten Gregory to drive. The chief mechanic was Bob Wallace who, some years later, was the chief development engineer and test driver for Lamborghini. They were sponsored by the Dow Chemical Company and they had a crew there making a film – very worthwhile for them as the car won the race. Our two cars had so many problems (including clutch problems on TOK) that we were well out of the hunt.

We then went to Le Mans where our entry was refused (see later).

Back in England we took part in a variety of GT races at Brands Hatch, Aintree (supporting the British Grand Prix), Snetterton and also the Tourist Trophy at Goodwood. The two Morgans were always at the "sharp end" of the 2 litre class and Chris and I put up some satisfactory performances. Our successes were very welcome at the factory in Malvern and plans were put in hand to produce a new car to be called the Plus Four Super Sports using a TR engine specially modified by Christopher's new company, Lawrencetune Engines, which had been formed as replacement to Westerham Motors. I well remember delivering two or three modified TR engines from Acton to Malvern in the firm's Standard 10 van and then returning with another three Triumph engines to be modified. It was not easy to tie them down in the back of the van and it made for an interesting time at roundabouts – I had to stop once or twice to shift them from one side to return some sort of stability to the vehicle!

As a "winter warmer" I competed in the Boxing Day meeting at Brands Hatch and had a fantastic "dice" with David Seigle-Morris in David Dixon's Austin-Healy 3000 (works prepared) which resulted in TOK winning and being 2nd overall in the GT race behind Peter Sargent's highly modified E-type Jaguar. It had snowed and frozen hard across the whole country so BBC TV had only this event to show and thus we had tremendous coverage – all very good publicity for Morgan (and the driver!)

For 1962 we then had a virtually new car with a lower 4/4 body which also carried the famous number TOK 258 – the forerunner for the new Super Sports model. Our first important race was back at Spa again and yet another 2nd place behind a Porsche Carrera-Abarth (average speed 104 mph – 167 kph). The first laps of the race were really quite tricky as it had rained before the start which left the road surface very slippery in the best Spa tradition. On the return leg back to the pits (this was the old 8 mile circuit on public roads) Hugh Braithwaite came off in a huge way and careered for a long distance across the fields before coming to rest amongst barbed-wire fences. His Morgan was a bit wrinkled but he escaped injury! We were again running the Le Mans 2.9 axle and I had a race-long "dice" with Bill Allen in the "works" Lotus Elite. We passed and re-passed many times, running extremely close together until I managed to open a bit of a gap in the final laps of the 120 mile race. "Pip" Arnold was 5th in his Plus Four, just behind Dieter Glemser in another Porsche Carrera.

On to the Nurburgring again where we should have tied up the 1600-2000 cc GT class but both cars had terrible problems with starter motors. They were over-heating underneath the exhaust manifolds and refusing to work after re-fuelling had taken place. Working on these delayed us far too much to gain a worthwhile result.

In 1961 we had been at Le Mans for the 24 Hours where we were accepted as an entry although we had originally only been on the reserve list. However, all sorts of political machinations took place and we were eventually thrown out and told "you've taken a 1930's car and added disc brakes to it – not in the spirit of the regulations. Go home!" The fact that XRX 1 was very obviously a brand new shiny car seemed lost on the Le Mans officials but, years later, we discovered that in fact the works Triumph team with their three twin-cam engined cars didn't want the possibility of being beaten by a Morgan with a push-rod Triumph engine so leant heavily on the ACO! Anyway, we said "we'll be back next year!".

For 1962 we had a fully confirmed entry from the Morgan Motor Company and went to the official test days at Le Mans in May during which we learned a huge amount about the car's performance, helping us to be far better prepared for the race in June. We had rain on the second day's test and, rather like Spa, the track surface with its deposit of rubber and oil from the daily traffic was extremely slippery.

I drove TOK to Le Mans for the test days as on our way from Berkshire to Dover with our motorhome we came across the caravan/transporter in a little lay-by in Redhill, Surrey. A chap was there holding a note from Christopher saying: "axle on caravan broken so have gone on with tools etc in the Jaguar. Please take TOK". So Penny and I left our two friends, John Adams and Pip Butler, to take the

Commer motorhome and we set off in TOK. French roads were not so good in those days; it was a bumpy and noisy trip there and back. Apart from the drivers in actual races, Penny probably held the record for the number of hours spent travelling as a passenger in a racing Morgan.

Back in England, the car was given a very thorough preparation which included fitting a "super special" starter motor from Lucas as well as incorporating heat shielding round the exhaust manifold above the starter motor. All the electrics were brought up to new specifications as were the braking system and suspension. As befitting a British entry, the car was re-sprayed in British Racing Green with the hard top in light grey to help with the sun's heat. It looked really smart and when you saw the factory's spare car, 170 GWP, in the same livery we were really well set up. In fact GWP was a "mobile spares department" – we used the screen from this car in the race as the original cracked in qualifying.

No problems at the technical inspection in 1962! We were greeted in a very friendly fashion by the ACO officials **this** time. One possible problem was ground clearance as all cars had to pass over a very high-tech measuring device – a box made from plywood! On the Dunlop racing tyres this was pretty marginal for TOK so that is why the photos taken during the inspection show the car on road rather than racing tyres. Every millimetre helped!

One important aspect of our team that is often overlooked in racing is that Chris and I were very evenly matched as to lap times – quite regularly turning in identical times in both qualifying and races. This enabled us to plan a very even pace for the car without overstressing anything. We were also physically very similar so there was no messing about at pit stops with different seats or cushions.

The long slow build up to the race was really rather nerve racking. It was very hot weather – well over 30 degrees. No rain – a wet 24 hour race is no fun at all. Chris started and was very fast away. We did 3 hour stints, based on the fuel consumption from the 90 litre tank. Taking over from Chris about 7pm on the Saturday was an emotional moment. Then – horror! – the starter motor failed to engage (thoughts of the Nurburging problem flashed into our minds). A quick turn on the end of the shaft by John Pierce and we were away. As one can imagine, the entire team's hearts were in their mouths in case this was history repeating itself. Not so, for the starter worked every time after that without problems. There was one more slight problem for one of the fuel filler caps (one to fill and one to breath to allow fast refuelling) was not closed properly after a stop and I was black flagged to come into the pits – a swift bang on the cap and off out again, much to my relief and also that of the two (anonymous) ACO official "fuel sealers" attached to our team for the race to ensure that the fuel caps were sealed after each re-fuelling.

As so many teams discover to their cost (and we see it at every Le Mans race) you succeed in long distance racing very often not on the track but by how long you spend in the pits – in our case a total of some 28 minutes in the 24 hours. That helped the average speed and distance covered – 2255 miles (3629 kms) at 94mph (151kph). Interestingly, if we had run TOK in every race since 1962 we would never have finished last ....a few years ago we would even have been 2nd in the 3-litre GT category and, in 2011, would not even have been last!

The Morgan, with a top speed on the Mulsanne straight of about 135mph (217kph) and 140-plus (225kph) into Indianapolis (slightly downhill) was not the slowest car in the race nor, naturally, the fastest. Consequently, when lining up to pass a little blue DB Panhard doing about 110mph (177kph) we had to be very careful that the red dot in the mirror wasn't a leading Ferrari doing some 180mph (290kph) plus! Imagine the consequences of blundering into their path ...we had to keep our wits about us. The long straights were not ideal Morgan territory but we fairly hared round the bends, often pulling away from much faster cars at these points. Great fun!

There was a group of Morgan enthusiast at Arnage who waved a Union Jack at us on every lap. Many years later I met them, saying that we had both certainly seen them and had waved back as their support was a great help.

The ACO had decided that there should be no more signals from the main pits in 1962 and there was a row of little "dug outs" just after the Mulsanne corner. These were connected to the main pits by field telephones – not entirely successfully. This outpost was very ably manned for us by Nigel Falconer and a chum, both of whom worked for the Rootes Group (later to become Chrysler and then Peugeot). However, the position of these signalling pits meant that if anything happened on the Mulsanne corner (like Mike Parkes getting his Ferrari into the sand on the exit!) then you missed the signal.

The car droned on happily but sounded a bit strange towards the end of the race as there was a split in the exhaust manifold. One strange thing was that there were only nineteen cars still running from the fifty-five that started so there were quite long periods when I never saw another car. The leading cars were so far in front that they were just cruising to the finish. I began to wonder – "have they all blown up, retired or crashed somewhere?" That is why the photographs showing the race finish have TOK all on its own with nothing else in sight. I did the final 3 hour run to the finish – very nerve-racking listening for any strange sounds from the car and also making sure I didn't make any silly mistakes to stop us finishing. The last lap was quite something and crossing the line at 4pm on Sunday afternoon was a huge moment for us all; the crowd seemed to love us – "le petit Morgan brave".

After the race finished the cars had to drive up to the end of the pits and then turn left and return to the Parc Ferme along the little track in front of the crowds. This was very difficult as there was virtually no travel left on the clutch pedal but I managed not to mow anyone down or hit another car. Les Fagg had jumped on to the back of the car just after the finish.

On Monday, the car was checked over, the plugs changed, the clutch adjusted and the exhaust fixed. Willy Edwards then drove the car back to England. I gather this was quite a trip with many hilarities and free drinks along the way! TOK had not been driven to Le Mans – it was carefully transported there in the caravan/transporter behind Chris' Jaguar Mk VII.

Other events back in England that summer included the August Bank Holiday meeting at Brands Hatch where Chris drove TOK to win the class using an engine built up by me – I can say that watching your engine race was far more stressful than actually racing oneself! We also went to Crystal Palace (right in a residential area of South London) for a GT race where TOK and GWP came first and second in their category. A difficult and rather dangerous circuit – no room for errors as there was a great deal of very hard scenery close to the track. Chris had a particular skill in the slow and medium speed corners at this circuit and, try as I might, I simply could not stay with him – this also applied to Snetterton, and Silverstone!

The last race for me in a Morgan was the Tourist Trophy at Goodwood in September. Again we had the two green cars and again we put up identical qualifying times. A lot of effort was put into "time and motion study" for the Le Mans-type start (the last one ever held in the UK). This paid off as we both made cracking getaways. GWP ran very well and I was running a clear third in the 2 litre class behind two Lotus Elites. Unfortunately a piston let go and that was that; although I had the consolation of setting a new 1301-2000cc class lap record of 1minutes 40.8 secs (85.71 mph). Chris went on to finish a fine 2nd in the class to Clive Hunt's Team Elite car.

An exciting and successful two years for us all with this Morgan project which certainly helped bring the Morgan Motor Company to the attention of many more people around the World. Chris and his team went on to develop the SLR cars, I stopped motor racing, joined Alfa Romeo and the other team members went about their different ways.

Dramatis personae in 1961 and 1962:

Drivers:
Christopher Lawrence, Richard Shepherd-Barron, Peter Marten, Bob Staples, Pip Arnold, Hugh Braithwaite

Team members:
Len Bridge, Les Fagg, John Harvey, Roland "Nobby" Smith, Willy Edwards, John Pierce

General helpers and also assistance at Le Mans:
Michael Billingham, John Jackson, Nigel Falconer, Tony Sanderson, Chris Ashmore (Le Mans re-fueller), Barry Staples, John Adams, and (from Morgan) Peter Morgan, George Goodall, Charlie Curtis.

And not forgetting those two absolute stalwarts – Jenny Lawrence and Penny Shepherd-Barron.

APPENDICES

TOK 258 TECHNICAL DETAILS

Specification: TOK 258 Morgan Plus 4

Type:
Morgan Plus 4 as built from 1952 to 1968. Cowled radiator model. The Plus 4 was the mainstay of Morgan's production during this period and was raced, rallied and trialled extensively.

Chassis:
Z Section steel with square section cross members

Body:
Aluminium alloy including the hardtop fitted to an ash wood frame

Engine:
Triumph TR3

Configuration:
Straight 4, wet liner, cast iron block & head

Valve mechanism:
2 valve pushrod

Lubrication:
Wet sump

Fuel system:
Twin Weber 42DCOE Carburretors

Ignition:
Lucas contact breaker

Engine capacity:
1991cc
Max output – 2002 – Approx 180bhp @ 6,250rpm
Max. output – 1962 – 138bhp @ 5,700rpm
Max. torque – 2002 – 140 ft lbs @ 5,750rpm
Max. torque – 1962 – 140ft lbs @ 3,800rpm

Exhaust system:
Lawrencetune tubular steel header

Cooling:
Standard Morgan brass radiator.
Electric fan. Oil cooler.

Fuel System:
100-litre fuel tank with two-pumps

Transmission:
Moss 4-speed gearbox
Morgan bell housing with AP racing single plate clutch
assembly

Steering:
Worm and peg steering box

Suspension:
Front: Morgan sliding pillar with coil springs and Koni
dampers
Rear: Solid axle with leaf springs and Koni dampers

Brakes:
Front: Girling 2 pot calliper disc brakes
Rear: Girling 9 inch drum brakes
Mintex: racing lining material front and rear

Wheels / Tyres:
15" x 6" front and rear Dunlop wire wheels.
Dunlop tyres

Weight:
Kerb weight – 800kgs

CHRISTOPHER LAWRENCE BIOGRAPHY

EDUCATION:
Pangbourne College
Royal Naval College, Dartmouth
Royal Naval Engineering College, Plymouth
Combined Universities Condensed BSc, 1953

CAREER – DESIGN & DEVELOPMENT:

1956
Rotacks MG Sports Racing Car

1960-68
Various versions of Deep Sanderson cars from single seater Formula Junior, two-seater sports racing coupés and road cars- including four examples which ran at Le Mans.

1964
Produced the now highly valued SLR Morgan Plus 4 with special racing bodywork with low drag

1966
Built the Cooper Ferrari F1 car for the new FIA 3-litre Formula, which was established in 1966. First F1 car with ventilated brake disks.

1968-74
Designer, developer and builder of the now much revered C.F.P.M. Monica 540 (only 40 ever built)

1986
Built the SL601 two-seater sports car for Bob Sutherland. This vehicle was produced in small numbers in Denver as the "Maxton"

1995
Responsible for chassis work on the 600LM Marcos GT cars which won the UK GT Championship and finished at Le Mans

1996
Employed by Morgan Motor Company to design and develop what is now the Aero 8. Spent two years racing in the FIA World GT Championship and the last three years developing the chassis for road use.

2001/02
Led Morgan's competitive return to Le Mans with the DEWALT/RSS team

CAREER – RACING:

Club racing

1958
Bought TOK 258 Morgan Plus 4 – "Marque" lap record at Goodwood

1959
Won 19 out of 22 races in Morgan Plus 4 to win the "Freddie DixonTrophy" in the National "Marque" Championship

1960
International 2-litre GT racing – lap record at Silverstone

1961
3rd Coppa InterEuropa, Monza, 3 hours

1962
Won 2-litre class at 24-hour Le Mans in TOK 258

1963
Won at Spa, Nurburgring, Dijon and Clermont-Ferrand Drove Deep Sanderson at Le Mans – led 1000cc class for 14 hours

1966
5 races in private F1 car made from a Cooper and a Ferrari engine. Won one point at German Grand Prix and came fifth in Oulton Park Gold Cup

1968
Led index of Thermal Efficiency, Le Mans in Deep Sanderson for 16 hours

1980
Moved to US and took up Classic and Vintage racing

1981-91
Won 55 races overall in the US in a variety of vehicles

1992
Returned to the UK. Occasionally raced old Morgans

2002
Drove TOK 258 in the 2002 Le Mans Classic

2005
June 16 – "Tribute to Chris Lawrence Day" at Goodwood Circuit

THE MORGAN CLUB OF HOLLAND COMMEMORATES TOK'S HISTORIC VICTORY

The Morgan Sports Car Club of Holland's event on 14/15 July 2012 at the Assen TT circuit celebrates the Morgan win at Le Mans in 1962. Morgan enthusiasts and personalities will be attending.

The club has produced a dedicated badge and posters for this event as shown below.

Machiel Kalf a senior member of the club and noted TOK 258 and Super Sports historian provided the collection of photos and memorabilia included in the appendix to this book.

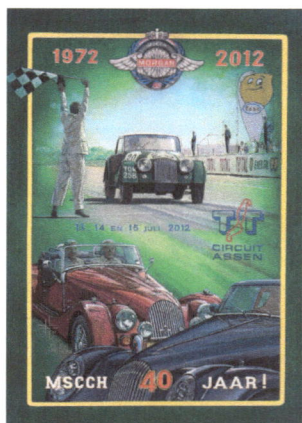

IMAGES AND DETAILS FROM 1962

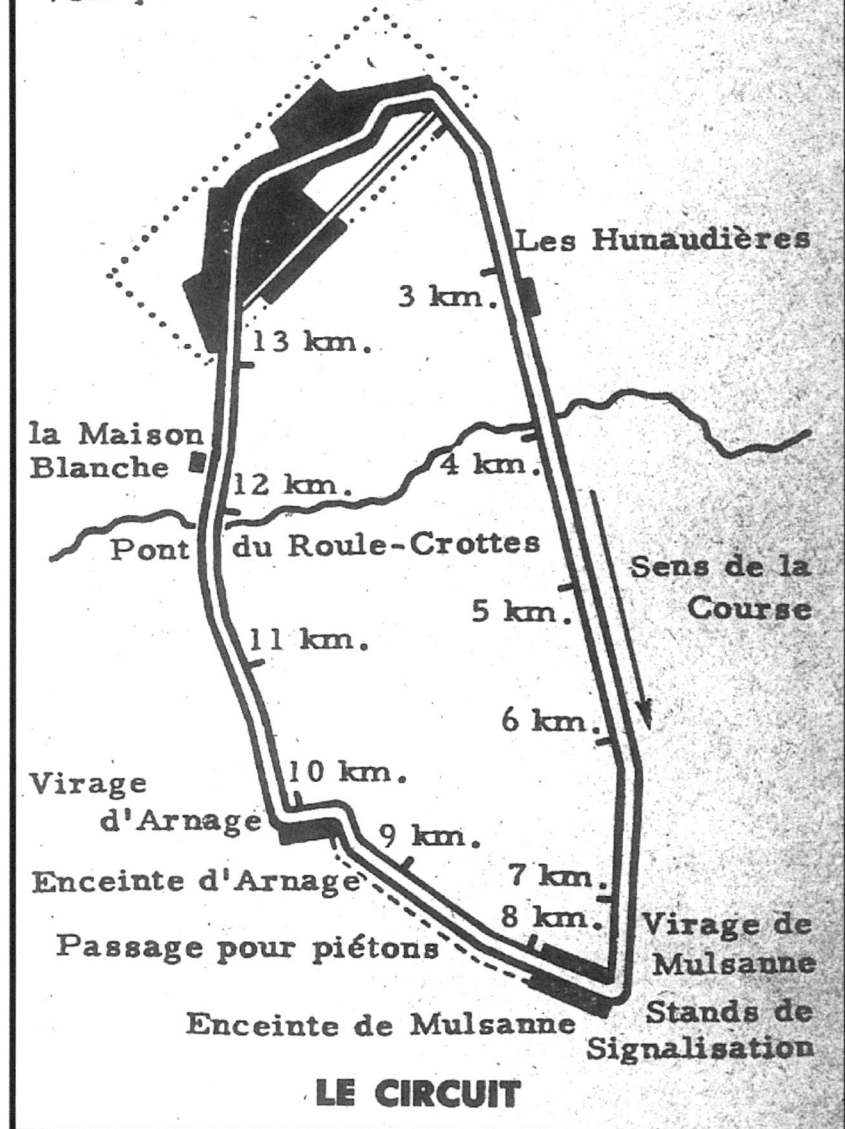

Voir plan détaillé page suivante

Les Hunaudières

3 km.

13 km.

la Maison Blanche

12 km.

4 km.

Pont du Roule-Crottes

Sens de la Course

5 km.

11 km.

6 km.

10 km.

Virage d'Arnage

9 km.

7 km.

Enceinte d'Arnage

8 km.

Passage pour piétons

Virage de Mulsanne

Stands de Signalisation

Enceinte de Mulsanne

LE CIRCUIT

LE MANS—How the cars finished   ■ ■ ■ SEE PAGES 2-5

RACE NO.	MAKE	DRIVERS	ENTRANT	Engine Position Front or Rear	No. of cylinders	Bore and Stroke (mm)	Capacity c.c.	Induction System	Brakes (Disc or Drum)	Tyres	Body Type and Category	Dry Weight (lb)	Finishing position or reason for Retirement	Laps Completed	Race average (mph)	Fastest Lap (mph)	Fastest Lap Speed min sec	Fastest Timed Speed along Straight (m.p.h.)	Actual Distance Covered Miles
1	Chevrolet Corv.	Settember-Turner	Sc. Scirocco	F	V-8	101.7×82.6	5359	Rochester F.I.	Drum	Dunlop	Closed-GT	2895	Piston	150	—	104.9	4 47.4	138	—
2	Maserati	Hansgen-McLaren	Cunningham	F	V-8	91×75.8	3944	4 D.C. Weber	Disc	Dunlop	Closed-Exp.	2144	Transmission	178	—	126.1	3 59.0	177	—
3	Maserati	Thompson-Kimberley	Cunningham	F	V-8	91×75.8	3944	4 D.C. Weber	Disc	Dunlop	Closed-Exp.	2160	Crashed	62	—	125.9	3 59.9	174	—
4	Ferrari	Trintignant-L. Bianchi	Maserati-France	F	V-12	77×71	3968	6 D.C. Weber	Disc	Dunlop	Open-Exp.	1990	Rear suspension	157	—	123.5	4 00.0	173	—
5	Ferrari	Parkes-Bandini	S.E.F.A.C.	F	V-12	77×71	3968	6 D.C. Weber	Disc	Dunlop	Open-Exp.	1990	FIRST	331	115.24	126.89	3 57.6	174	2765.0
6	Ferrari	Charles-Coundley	S.E.F.A.C.	F	6-in-line	87×106	3781	3 D.C. Weber	Disc	Dunlop	Closed-G.T.	2630	Overheating	56	—	123.4	3 .7	171	—
7	Jaguar	Sargent	Charles	F	6-in-line	87×106	3781	3 D.C. Weber	Disc	Dunlop	Closed-G.T.	2470	No oil	53	—	121.3	4 25.0	174	—
8	Jaguar	Cunningham-Salvadori	Sargent	F	6-in-line	87×106	3781	3 D.C. Weber	Disc	Dunlop	Closed-G.T.	2320	FIFTH	310	107.79	118.8	4 13.0	168	2587.0
9	Jaguar	G. Hill-Ginther	Cunningham	F	6-in-line	96×92	3996	3 D.C. Weber	Disc	Dunlop	Closed-G.T.	2306	FOURTH	310	107.87	121.9	—	168	2589.1
10	Aston Martin	Kerguen—Franc	Kerguen	F	6-in-line	93×92	3749	3 D.C. Weber	Disc	Dunlop	Closed-G.T.	2344	Head Gasket	78	—	121.9	3 03.3	168	—
11	Aston Martin	Salmon-Baillie	Salmon	F	6-in-line	93×92	3749	3 D.C. Weber	Disc	Dunlop	Closed-G.T.	2344	Brakes, oil pipe	134	—	115.7	4 08.9	160	—
12	Aston Martin	Bonnier-Gurney	S.S.S.R. de Venice	F	V-12	73×58.8	2953	6 D.C. Weber	Disc	Dunlop	Closed-G.T.	2456	Head Gasket	124	—	115.6	4 20.8	155	—
13	Ferrari	Abate-C. Davis	S.S.S.R. de Venice	F	V-12	73×58.8	2953	6 D.C. Weber	Disc	Dunlop	Closed-G.T.	1788	Pistons	30	—	122.9	3 03.0	168	—
14	Ferrari	Grossman-Roberts	S.S.S.R. de Venice	F	V-12	73×58.8	2953	6 D.C. Weber	Disc	Dunlop	Closed-G.T.	1816	Transmission	30	—	123.1	3 08.0	161	—
15	Ferrari	Fulp-Ryan	N.A.R.T.	F	V-12	73×58.8	2953	6 D.C. Weber	Disc	Goodyear	Closed-G.T.	2060	Transmission	20	—	123.3	3 03.0	163	—
16	Ferrari	Noblet-Guichet	Noblet	F	V-12	73×58.8	2953	6 D.C. Weber	Disc	Dunlop	Closed-G.T.	2200	Clutch	297	103.50	119.9	3 59.1	163	2482.6
17	Ferrari	Ireland-Gregory	N.A.R.T.	F	V-12	73×58.8	2953	6 D.C. Weber	Disc	Goodyear	Closed-Exp.	2190	Clutch	2	—	125.7	4 04.6	159	—
18	Ferrari	Hyman-Reed	U.D.T.-Laystall	F	V-12	73×58.8	2953	6 D.C. Weber	Disc	Dunlop	Closed-G.T.	2220	Dynamo	325	101.51	123.3	3 59.7	158	2724.2
19	Ferrari	Hugus	Hugus	F	V-12	73×58.9	2958	3 D.C. Weber	Disc	Dunlop	Closed-G.T.	2190	NINTH	311	97.85	106.8	4 06.8	156	2348.3
20	Ferrari	Fido-Beurlys	E.N. Belge	F	V-12	73×58.8	2953	6 D.C. Weber	Disc	Dunlop	Closed-G.T.	2220	SECOND	302	109.10	121.0	3 .6	155	2618.4
21	Ferrari	Tavano-Simon	Tavano	F	6-in-line	94×89.7	2495	3 D.C. Weber	Disc	Dunlop	Closed-G.T.	1640	Overheating	211	—	116.2	4 19.0	159	—
22	Austin-Healey	Olthoff-Whitmore	Ecurie-Chiltern	F	6-in-line	83×92	2645	2 Zenith	D.F/D.r.R	Dunlop	Closed-G.T.	2332	Pistons	81	—	122.1	4 45.2	162	—
23	Ferrari	P. and R. Rodriguez	Ecurie Écosse	R	V-6	85×71	2418	2 D.C. Weber	Disc	Dunlop	Closed-Exp.	1697	Transmission	230	—	123.3	4 04.5	162	—
24	Ferrari	Lawrence-S. Barrow	S.E.F.A.C.	R	Flat-4	85×71	1588	2 D.C. Weber	Disc	Dunlop	Open-Exp.	1570	Transmission	175	—	135.4	3 57.2	—	—
25	Ferrari	Bolton-Sanderson	Morgan Motor Co.	F	Flat-4	82×66	1582	2 D.C. Solex	Drum	Pirelli	Closed-G.T.	1285	Transmission	270	93.96	101.8	4 02.1	130	—
26	Morgan	Harper-Procter	Porsche	R	Flat-4	82×66	1582	2 Zenith	Disc	Pirelli	Closed-G.T.	2090	No Water	35	—	97.2	5 57.9	—	—
27	T.V.R.	Hopkirk-Jopp	T.V.R. Cars	R	Flat-4	81×57.8	1590	2 D.C. Weber	Disc	Pirelli	Closed-G.T.	2088	FIFTEENTH	268	93.24	99.5	4 .6	118	2237.8
28	Sunbeam Alpine	Buchi-Herrmann	Sunbeam Talbot	R	Flat-4	81×57.8	1590	2 D.C. Weber	Disc	Dunlop	Closed-G.T.	1775	Engine Bearings	187	—	98.4	4 .6	142	—
29	Sunbeam Alpine	Barth-Schiller	Sunbeam Talbot	F	4-in-line	87.5×66	1592	2 D.C. Solex	Disc	Dunlop	Closed-G.T.	1790	TWELFTH	287	100.90	106.6	4 .0	129	2309.76
30	Porsche	Veuillet	Veuillet	R	4-in-line	80×57.8	1569	2 D.C. Weber	Disc	Dunlop	Closed-G.T.	1740	No Water	13	—	104.9	4 47.5	140	—
31	Osca	Bentley-Gordon	Osca	F	4-in-line	80×78	1568	2 D.C. Weber	Disc	Pirelli	Closed-Exp.	1740	SEVENTEENTH	272	94.45	97.9	4 07.8	—	2271.5
32	Osca	Behra-Arents	Osca	F	4-in-line	78×75×615	1569	2 D.C. Weber	Disc	Pirelli	Closed-Exp.	1795	Camshaft	85	—	98.6	4 19.5	—	—
33	Marcos	Hine-Frost	Marcos	F	4-in-line	78×75	1562	2 Zenith	Disc	Dunlop	Closed-G.T.	1755	No Water	227	—	99.5	4 .0	129	—
34	Alfa-Romeo	Sala-De Luca	Sc. Sc. Ambrosiana	F	4-in-line	74×75	1290	2 D.C. Weber	Disc	Pirelli	Closed-Exp.	1762	TENTH	281	97.73	100.6	4 04.1	129	—
35	Alfa-Romeo	Foitek-Ricci	Sc. Sc. Ambrosiana	F	4-in-line	74×75	1290	2 D.C. Weber	Disc	Pirelli	Closed-Exp.	1514	Clutch	60	—	103.3	4 49.0	135	—
36	Abarth-Simca	De Lageneste-Rolland	Abarth Corse	R	4-in-line	76×71	1288	2 D.C. Weber	Disc	Michelin X	Closed-Exp.	1488	Valve & Pistons	21	—	103.1	4 57.8	129	—
37	Abarth-Simca	Orrdier-Spychiger	Abarth Corse	R	4-in-line	76×71	1288	2 D.C. Weber	Disc	Michelin X	Closed-Exp.	1488	Gearbox	71	—	106.2	4 41.8	131	—
38	Abarth-Simca	Deboli-Harris	Abarth Corse	R	4-in-line	76×71	1288	2 D.C. Weber	Disc	Dunlop	Closed-Exp.	1516	EIGHTH	268	93.29	106.5	4 42.8	130	2238.9
39	Lotus Elite	Hobbs-Gardner	Lotus Eng.	F	4-in-line	76.2×66.67	1216	2 S.U.	Disc	Dunlop	Closed-G.T.	1286	FOURTH	286	89.60	95.4	4 61.8	129	2390.4
40	Lotus Elite	Hunt-Wylie	Lotus Eng.	F	4-in-line	76.2×66.67	1216	2 S.U.	Disc	Dunlop	Closed-G.T.	1278	SIXTH	278	88.59	97.5	5 02.2	127	2319.8
41	René Bonnet	Consten-Rousiui	Autom. R. Bonnet	R	4-in-line	64.5×54	706	2 D.C. Weber	Disc	Michelin	Closed-Exp.	355	THIRTEENTH	255	86.59	94.6	5 .4	123	2319.0
42	René Bonnet	Armagnac-Laureau	Autom. R. Bonnet	R	4-in-line	64.5×54	701	2 D.C. Weber	Disc	Michelin	Closed-Exp.	355	ELEVENTH	255	87.95	95.7	5 02.2	112	2126.0
43	Fiat Abarth	Fraissinet-Condrillier	Abarth Corse	R	4-in-line	61.23×59.5	701	2 D.C. Weber	Disc	Pirelli	Closed-Exp.	1365	SIXTEENTH	255	—	94.6	5 15.4	118	2100.2
44	Fiat Abarth	DLanesi-M. Bianchi	Abarth Corse	R	4-in-line	61.23×59.5	701	1 D.C. Weber	Disc	Pirelli	Closed-Exp.	180	Valves	17	—	91.0	5 30.8	118	—
45	Fiat Abarth CD	Letelong-Heurtoud	Panhard	F	Flat-2	77×75	702	1 D.C. Weber	Disc	Michelin	Closed-Exp.	192	Crashed	128	—	92.8	5 24.2	113	—
46	Panhard CD	Boyer-Verrier	Panhard	F	Flat-2	77×75	702	1 Zenith	Drum	Michelin	Closed-Exp.	355	—	—	—	—	—	—	—
47	Panhard CD	Vinatier-Bobit	S.S.S.R. De Venise	F	V-12	73×58.8	2953	2 D.C. Weber	Disc	Goodyear	Closed-G.T.	2204	Crashed	172	—	92.8	5 30.6	118	2129.4
48	Ferrari	Berger-Darville	E.N. Belge	F	6-in-line	66×96	706	1 D.C. Weber	Disc	Goodyear	Closed-Exp.	1750	Clutch	49	—	116.0	4 19.7	160	—
49	A.C. Bristol	Magg-Martin	Autom. R. Bonnet	R	4-in-line	64.5×54	706	3 D.C. Weber	D.F/D.r.R	Pirelli	Closed-Exp.	1488	Rear suspension	13	—	91.3	5 .9	124	—
50	Abarth Simca	Sutrunini-Albert	Abarth Corse	R	4-in-line	76×71	1288	2 D.C. Weber	Disc	Pirelli	Closed-Exp.	—	—	30	—	—	—	—	—

THE *Morgan* PLUS 4 & 4/4 SERIES IV

LE MANS 1962

First in the 2 litre Grand Touring Class. During the 24 hours the car averaged a speed of 94 m.p.h.

1962-63 PRICES

MODEL		BASIC PRICE	PURCHASE TAX			TOTAL		
4/4	Series IV	£545	£205	7	9	£750	7	9
PLUS 4	Two Seater	£675	£254	2	9	£929	2	9
PLUS 4	Four Seater	£690	£259	15	3	£949	15	3
PLUS 4	D.H. Coupé	£730	£274	15	3	£1004	15	3
PLUS 4	Super Sports	£925	£347	17	9	£1272	17	9

United Kingdom Agents

Basil Roy Ltd.,
161 Great Portland Street,
LONDON, W.1.

Johnson & Brown,
268-270 High Street,
BROMLEY,
Kent.

Rossleigh Ltd.,
43/45 Lothian Road,
EDINBURGH.

Bolton of Leeds Ltd.,
14 Harrison Street,
Briggate,
LEEDS, 1,
Yorks.

Lifes Motors Ltd.,
32-36 West Street,
SOUTHPORT,
Lancs.

Kingsley Park Garage,
Kingsley Park Terrace,
NORTHAMPTON.

Cedar Motor House,
110-112 Bath Road,
CHELTENHAM,
Glos.

Bowman & Acock Ltd.,
Pickersleigh Garage,
MALVERN LINK,
Worcs.

Husham's (Cars) Ltd.,
Penn Hill Garage,
PARKSTONE,
Dorset.

Westleigh Garage Ltd.,
1339 London Road,
LEIGH-ON-SEA,
Essex.

E. W. Burnett & Sons,
5 Eldon Street,
SOUTHSEA.

Playing Place Motors,
TRURO,
Cornwall.

MORGAN MOTOR CO. LTD.

PICKERSLEIGH ROAD, MALVERN LINK, WORCESTERSHIRE, ENGLAND.

AUTOMOBILE·CLUB DE L'OUEST

23·24   JUIN   1962

Image courtesy of Machiel Kalf (The Morgan Sports Car Club of Holland)

XXXᵉ GRAND PRIX D'ENDURANCE

LES 24 HEURES DU MANS

23-24 JUIN
1962

ORGANISÉ PAR L'ASSOCIATION SPORTIVE DE L'AUTOMOBILE-CLUB DE L'OUEST

Image courtesy of Machiel Kalf (The Morgan Sports Car Club of Holland)

Automobile-Club de l'Ouest

LES 24 HEURES DU MANS

23 et 24 Juin 1962

TABLEAU de POINTAGE
=== OFFICIEL ===

N° 003875

**Seul autorisé
Prix : 2 NF**

ATTENTION

Ce Tableau de pointage officiel
numéroté peut vous permettre de **GAGNER**

1° - Un Téléviseur **Schneider**

2° - Une Montre **Lip** (plaquée or)

IMPORTANT - Le tirage aura lieu à la BOURSE
de COMMERCE, Lundi 25 Juin 1962 à 16 heures.

Édité par « LA PUBLICITÉ GÉNÉRALE », Maurice RAMADE, Directeur
(38ᵉ année), 72 bis, rue de la Mariette, LE MANS - Tél. 28-09-87

Programme cover

Image courtesy of Machiel Kalf (The Morgan Sports Car Club of Holland)

CHAMPIONNAT DU MONDE
DE GRAND TOURISME

BELIGOND

24 Heures du Mans 1962

PRIX DU PROGRAMME : 3,50 NF

AVEC CE PROGRAMME, VOUS POUVEZ GAGNER UNE **SIMCA 1.000**
OU UN SCOOTER **VESPA**, OU UN BRIQUET *SILVER-MATCH*
OU UNE CAMÉRA **KODAK**, OU UNE MONTRE **LIP**

Voir
aussi
page 6

N° 001751

Image courtesy of Machiel Kalf (The Morgan Sports Car Club of Holland)

Press pass

Les 24 Heures du Mans
23 et 24 Juin 1962

1962

PRESSE

Cette carte doit être portée ostensiblement.

Image courtesy of Machiel Kalf (The Morgan Sports Car Club of Holland)

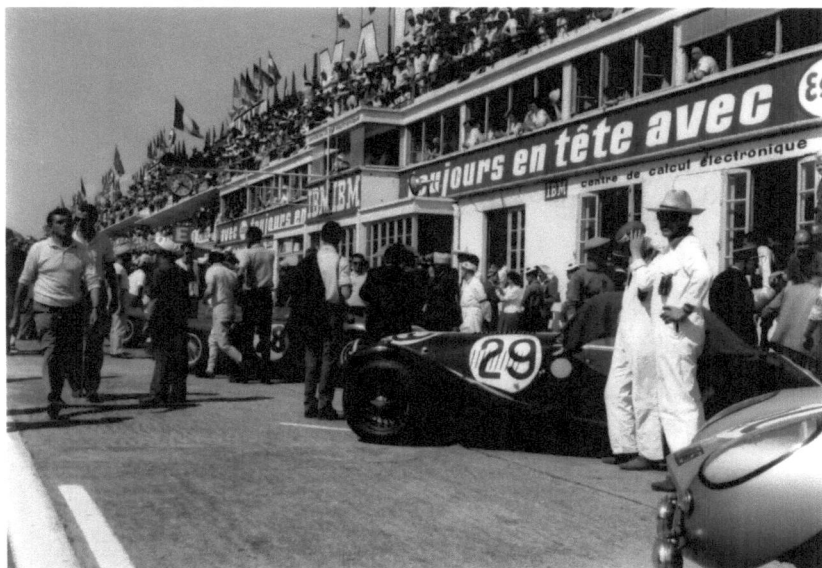

Images courtesy of Machiel Kalf (The Morgan Sports Car Club of Holland)

Image courtesy of Machiel Kalf (The Morgan Sports Car Club of Holland)

Richard and Chris at the technical inspection in 1962

TOK in the rain during the test days

Image courtesy of Machiel Kalf (The Morgan Sports Car Club of Holland)

Both drivers confirmed how well TOK cornered, wet & dry

Image courtesy of Machiel Kalf (The Morgan Sports Car Club of Holland)

30ᵐᵉ GRAND PRIX D'ENDURANCE
DE 24 HEURES

IBM
FRANCE

(23-24 JUIN 1962)

CLASSEMENT A LA DISTANCE 10 **HEURE**

CLASSEMENT	N° VOITURE	MARQUE VOITURE	Nbre de TOURS	HEURE DE PASSAGE			
				H	M	S	1/10
1	06	FERRARI	226	15	55	46	0
2	27	FERRARI	221	15	56	41	6
3	19	FERRARI	216	15	57	26	1
4	17	FERRARI	216	15	57	54	3
5	22	FERRARI	210	15	57	39	3
6	09	JAGUAR	205	15	56	38	1
7	10	JAGUAR	200	15	57	54	4
8	24	AUSTIN HEALEY	190	15	55	55	2
9	21	FERRARI	191	15	00	27	5
10	44	LOTUS ELITE	151	15	55	24	5
11	34	PORSCHE	165	15	59	15	4
12	35	ALFA ROMEO	117	15	47	27	7
13	45	LOTUS ELITE	182	15	55	58	6
14	28	MORGAN	179	15	58	41	3
15	38	SUNBEAM	178	15	58	00	4
16	40	ALFA ROMEO	177	15	57	53	2
17	37	OSCA	176	15	58	55	0
18	55	PORSCHE	175	15	57	17	6
19	43	ABARTH SIMCA	172	15	59	05	8
20	55	FIAT ABARTH	170	15	59	29	1
21	45	BONNET	164	15	56	26	6
22	53	PANHARD	188	15	56	51	6
23	33	SUNBEAM	187	15	55	02	1
24	50	BONNET	155	15	56	11	9

TOK 258 TODAY

One of the fascinating aspects of the TOK saga is that this famous car lives on not just resting in a motorsport museum but participating actively in a range of events, including historic racing in the capable hands of Keith Ahlers who now owns TOK.

Back in early 2000 TOK had just completed a total rebuild by Rick Bourne which was praised by Chris Lawrence for its quality. He and Rick Bourne did parade laps before the 2002 Le Mans race.

The following photos depicting TOK in a range of recent activities were provided by Roger Tatton the MSCC archivist – who also supplied the captions.

By the famous cow sheds on the Le Mans Expo camp site

TOK entering the main track from the Bugatti Circuit assembly point at the Le Mans Classic 2006.

TOK with one of the 80 Le Mans 1962 limited edition cars

TOK in the display area at Mog 2011, Newmarket

THE AUTHORS

Ronnie Price

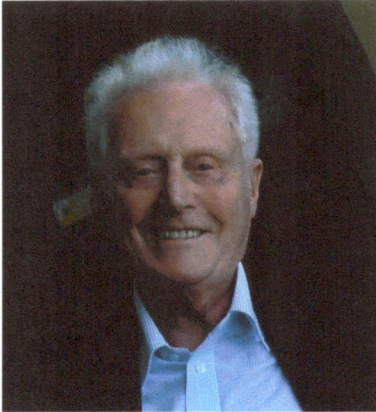

Ronnie Price puts his life long love of cars and motor-racing down to the fact that he was born in Coventry – where major motor manufacturing began around 120 years ago.

He has owned Jaguars, MGs, a Riley and a plethora of other vehicles; and engaged in extremely modest sporting activity including local rallies and minor hill climbs.

It was when he achieved a long time ambition to own a Morgan that he first became fascinated by the TOK story. He tried to find a book dedicated to TOK's Le Mans win, not simply references in Morgan histories. Since there wasn't one, he decided to write the story. He felt TOK deserved it.

Richard Shepherd-Barron

Richard Shepherd-Barron started motor-racing in 1958 with a Fiat-Abarth 750 in club and national events in England and Scotland. In 1959, he progressed to an Alfa Romeo Giulietta Sprint Veloce, running in 42 events in the 1300 and 1600cc GT classes again in England and Scotland but at Spa and Monza also. 1960 was again with the Alfa plus Formula Junior in Italy and England and sharing Bob Staples' AC Ace-Bristol at the Nurburgring 1,000 km. Meeting Chris Lawrence at this event proved a critical point and he joined him for the next two years with the Morgan Plus Four Super Sports TOK 258, XRX I and 170 GWP – many successful GT races in England as well as Spa and Nurburgring, with the 1962 Le Mans class win in TOK. Richard then stopped racing to join Alfa Romeo and help establish their UK subsidiary. Today, he lives in Suffolk and writes for business, farming and motoring magazines.

Also from MX Publishing

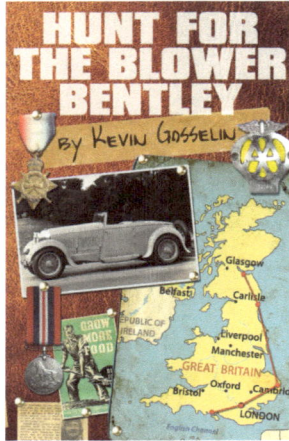

"It's pure magic if you are a car man or woman. It's not a whodunit, more of a whereisit, and each chapter jumps between the war years in Britain to the present, telling the tale of Bentley chassis number SM3912"

Brian Johnson (lead singer AC/DC)
in **Octane Magazine**

Also available from MX Publishing

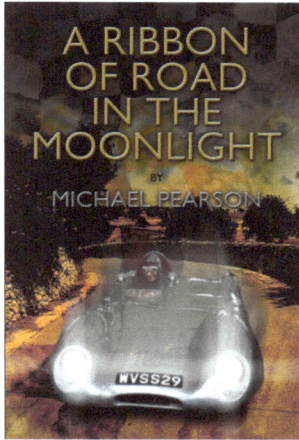

The story concerns Mike Brookes and his Pegasus Car Company as they attempt to build and enter a two car team for the 1957 Targa Florio road race in Sicily. Pegasus build road-going sports cars but Brookes wants to take them onto an international stage to compete with the likes of Ferrari, Maserati, and Mercedes. He selects the Targa Florio as it is the toughest road race in the world, combining a car breaking mountain section with a long flat-out 180mph straight.

"Kept me entertained for several hours. I'll pass the book on to my gearhead friends"
Amazon Review

www.ingramcontent.com/pod-product-compliance
Lightning Source LLC
Chambersburg PA
CBHW051238090426
42742CB00001B/11